# 50 Classic American Diner Recipes for Home

By: Kelly Johnson

# Table of Contents

- Pancakes with maple syrup
- Cheeseburger with fries
- Blueberry pancakes
- Club sandwich
- French toast
- Reuben sandwich
- Chicken and waffles
- BLT sandwich
- Corned beef hash
- Monte Cristo sandwich
- Denver omelette
- Philly cheesesteak
- Biscuits and gravy
- Tuna melt sandwich
- Eggs Benedict
- Patty melt
- Western omelette
- Meatloaf with mashed potatoes
- Grilled cheese sandwich
- Huevos Rancheros
- Turkey club sandwich
- Chicken fried steak with gravy
- Chili cheese fries
- Breakfast burrito
- Fish and chips
- Fried chicken and biscuits
- Chicken pot pie
- Cobb salad
- Chicken Caesar salad
- Macaroni and cheese
- Vegetable omelette
- Classic burger with lettuce, tomato, and onion
- Shrimp Po' Boy sandwich
- Spinach and feta omelette
- Hot roast beef sandwich with gravy

- Cobb salad
- Turkey burger with sweet potato fries
- Greek salad
- Classic meatloaf sandwich
- Chicken Caesar wrap
- Grilled salmon with steamed vegetables
- Meatball sub
- Greek omelette
- Classic tuna salad sandwich
- BBQ pulled pork sandwich
- Cobb salad wrap
- Spinach and mushroom omelette
- Veggie burger with coleslaw
- Steak and eggs
- Classic chocolate milkshake

**Pancakes with maple syrup**

Ingredients:

- 1 cup all-purpose flour
- 2 tablespoons granulated sugar
- 1 teaspoon baking powder
- 1/2 teaspoon baking soda
- 1/4 teaspoon salt
- 1 cup buttermilk (or substitute with 1 cup milk mixed with 1 tablespoon lemon juice or vinegar, let sit for 5 minutes)
- 1 large egg
- 2 tablespoons melted butter or vegetable oil
- Butter or oil for cooking
- Maple syrup, for serving

Instructions:

In a large mixing bowl, whisk together the flour, sugar, baking powder, baking soda, and salt until well combined.
In a separate bowl, beat the egg, then add the buttermilk and melted butter or oil. Whisk until well combined.
Pour the wet ingredients into the dry ingredients and stir until just combined. Do not overmix; a few lumps are okay. Let the batter rest for about 5-10 minutes.
Heat a non-stick skillet or griddle over medium heat. Add a small amount of butter or oil to coat the surface.
Pour about 1/4 cup of batter onto the skillet for each pancake. Cook until bubbles form on the surface of the pancake and the edges begin to look set, about 2-3 minutes.
Flip the pancake and cook until golden brown on the other side, about 1-2 minutes more.
Remove the pancake from the skillet and repeat with the remaining batter, adding more butter or oil to the skillet as needed.
Serve the pancakes warm with maple syrup drizzled over the top. You can also add additional toppings like fresh berries, sliced bananas, or chopped nuts if desired.

Enjoy your homemade pancakes with maple syrup for a classic diner-style breakfast treat!

**Cheeseburger with fries**

Cheeseburger Ingredients:

- 1 lb (450g) ground beef (preferably 80/20 blend)
- Salt and pepper, to taste
- 4 hamburger buns
- 4 slices of cheese (cheddar, American, or your choice)
- Optional toppings: lettuce, tomato, onion, pickles, ketchup, mustard, mayonnaise

Fries Ingredients:

- 4 large potatoes (russet or Idaho), washed and dried
- 2-3 tablespoons olive oil
- Salt, to taste
- Optional seasoning: paprika, garlic powder, onion powder, or your preferred seasoning blend

Instructions:

1. Prepare the Fries:

    Preheat your oven to 425°F (220°C).
    Cut the potatoes into thin strips or wedges, about 1/4 inch thick.
    In a large bowl, toss the potato strips with olive oil until evenly coated.
    Season the potatoes with salt and any additional seasoning of your choice, tossing to coat evenly.
    Spread the seasoned potato strips in a single layer on a baking sheet lined with parchment paper or aluminum foil.
    Bake in the preheated oven for 25-30 minutes, flipping halfway through, until the fries are golden brown and crispy.

2. Prepare the Cheeseburgers:

    Preheat a grill or skillet over medium-high heat.
    Divide the ground beef into 4 equal portions and shape them into burger patties.
    Season both sides of each patty with salt and pepper.
    Cook the burger patties on the grill or skillet for about 4-5 minutes per side, or until desired level of doneness is reached.

During the last minute of cooking, top each burger patty with a slice of cheese and allow it to melt.
Toast the hamburger buns on the grill or in a toaster until lightly golden.
Assemble the cheeseburgers by placing a cooked patty with melted cheese on the bottom half of each bun.
Add your desired toppings, such as lettuce, tomato, onion, pickles, ketchup, mustard, or mayonnaise.
Place the top half of the bun over the toppings to complete the cheeseburgers.

3. Serve:

Serve the cheeseburgers hot alongside the crispy fries.
Enjoy your delicious homemade cheeseburgers with fries!

Feel free to customize your cheeseburgers with your favorite toppings and condiments to suit your taste preferences.

**Blueberry pancakes**

Ingredients:

- 1 cup all-purpose flour
- 2 tablespoons granulated sugar
- 1 teaspoon baking powder
- 1/2 teaspoon baking soda
- 1/4 teaspoon salt
- 1 cup buttermilk (or substitute with 1 cup milk mixed with 1 tablespoon lemon juice or vinegar, let sit for 5 minutes)
- 1 large egg
- 2 tablespoons melted butter or vegetable oil
- 1/2 teaspoon vanilla extract (optional)
- 1/2 cup fresh or frozen blueberries
- Butter or oil for cooking
- Maple syrup, for serving

Instructions:

In a large mixing bowl, whisk together the flour, sugar, baking powder, baking soda, and salt until well combined.

In a separate bowl, beat the egg, then add the buttermilk, melted butter or oil, and vanilla extract (if using). Whisk until well combined.

Pour the wet ingredients into the dry ingredients and stir until just combined. Do not overmix; a few lumps are okay. Let the batter rest for about 5-10 minutes.

Gently fold in the blueberries into the pancake batter.

Heat a non-stick skillet or griddle over medium heat. Add a small amount of butter or oil to coat the surface.

Pour about 1/4 cup of batter onto the skillet for each pancake. Cook until bubbles form on the surface of the pancake and the edges begin to look set, about 2-3 minutes.

Flip the pancake and cook until golden brown on the other side, about 1-2 minutes more.

Remove the pancake from the skillet and repeat with the remaining batter, adding more butter or oil to the skillet as needed.

Serve the blueberry pancakes warm with maple syrup drizzled over the top. You can also add additional toppings like extra blueberries, whipped cream, or a dusting of powdered sugar if desired.

Enjoy your homemade blueberry pancakes for a delicious and satisfying breakfast!

**Club sandwich**

Ingredients:

- 3 slices of bread (toasted)
- 2-3 slices of cooked bacon
- 2-3 slices of roasted turkey breast
- 2-3 slices of cooked ham
- 1 leaf of lettuce
- 1 ripe tomato, sliced
- Mayonnaise
- Toothpicks (for securing the sandwich)

Instructions:

Toast the bread slices until golden brown and crispy.
Lay out one slice of toasted bread on a clean surface. Spread a thin layer of mayonnaise over the top side.
Layer the first slice with one leaf of lettuce and a couple of tomato slices.
Place another slice of toasted bread on top of the tomato slices. Spread mayonnaise on one side of this slice.
Layer this slice with the cooked bacon slices, followed by the slices of roasted turkey breast.
Place the third slice of toasted bread on top of the turkey. Spread mayonnaise on one side of this slice.
Layer this slice with the cooked ham slices.
Carefully place the top layer of the sandwich onto the ham layer, mayonnaise side down.
Secure the Club Sandwich with toothpicks, inserting them at even intervals across the sandwich.
Use a sharp knife to slice the sandwich diagonally into halves or quarters.
Serve the Club Sandwich immediately, either as a whole or with a side of fries, chips, or a crisp pickle.

Feel free to customize your Club Sandwich by adding cheese slices, avocado, or your favorite condiments. Enjoy this iconic diner classic for lunch or a hearty snack!

**French toast**

Ingredients:

- 4 slices of bread (thick slices such as brioche, challah, or Texas toast work well)
- 2 large eggs
- 1/2 cup milk (whole milk or any milk of your choice)
- 1 teaspoon vanilla extract
- 1/2 teaspoon ground cinnamon (optional)
- Butter or oil for cooking
- Maple syrup, powdered sugar, or your favorite toppings for serving

Instructions:

In a shallow dish or bowl, whisk together the eggs, milk, vanilla extract, and ground cinnamon until well combined.
Heat a non-stick skillet or griddle over medium heat and add a small amount of butter or oil to coat the surface.
Dip each slice of bread into the egg mixture, ensuring both sides are coated but not overly soaked.
Place the dipped bread slices onto the heated skillet or griddle.
Cook the French toast for 2-3 minutes on each side, or until golden brown and cooked through.
Remove the cooked French toast from the skillet and transfer to a plate.
Repeat the dipping and cooking process with the remaining slices of bread.
Serve the French toast warm with maple syrup, powdered sugar, or your favorite toppings.

Feel free to customize your French toast by adding sliced fruits, whipped cream, nuts, or a sprinkle of cinnamon on top. Enjoy this comforting and delicious breakfast treat!

**Reuben sandwich**

Ingredients:

- 8 slices of rye bread
- 1/2 lb (225g) thinly sliced corned beef
- 1 cup sauerkraut, drained
- 4 slices Swiss cheese
- 1/4 cup Russian dressing (store-bought or homemade)
- Butter or margarine, softened

Russian Dressing Ingredients:

- 1/2 cup mayonnaise
- 2 tablespoons ketchup
- 1 tablespoon sweet pickle relish
- 1 teaspoon Worcestershire sauce
- 1/2 teaspoon paprika
- 1/4 teaspoon garlic powder
- Salt and pepper, to taste

Instructions:

1. Make Russian Dressing (if not using store-bought):

    In a small bowl, combine mayonnaise, ketchup, sweet pickle relish, Worcestershire sauce, paprika, garlic powder, salt, and pepper. Stir until well combined. Adjust seasoning to taste. Set aside.

2. Assemble the Reuben Sandwiches:

    Lay out 4 slices of rye bread on a clean surface.
    Spread Russian dressing on one side of each slice of bread.
    Top each slice of bread with an equal amount of corned beef, followed by sauerkraut and a slice of Swiss cheese.
    Place the remaining 4 slices of rye bread on top of each sandwich to complete the assembly.

3. Grill the Reuben Sandwiches:

>Heat a large skillet or griddle over medium heat.
>Spread softened butter or margarine on the outsides of each sandwich.
>Place the sandwiches on the skillet or griddle and cook until the bread is golden brown and the cheese is melted, about 3-4 minutes per side.
>Press down on the sandwiches gently with a spatula while cooking to help the ingredients meld together.

4. Serve:

>Remove the Reuben sandwiches from the skillet or griddle and transfer to a cutting board.
>Use a sharp knife to slice each sandwich in half diagonally.
>Serve hot with a side of pickles, coleslaw, or potato chips, if desired.

Enjoy the classic flavors of the Reuben sandwich with its savory corned beef, tangy sauerkraut, and creamy Russian dressing!

**Chicken and waffles**

Ingredients:

For the Fried Chicken:

- 4 boneless, skinless chicken breasts
- 1 cup all-purpose flour
- 1 teaspoon salt
- 1/2 teaspoon black pepper
- 1/2 teaspoon paprika
- 1/4 teaspoon garlic powder
- 2 eggs, beaten
- Vegetable oil for frying

For the Waffles:

- 2 cups all-purpose flour
- 2 tablespoons granulated sugar
- 1 tablespoon baking powder
- 1/2 teaspoon salt
- 1 3/4 cups milk
- 1/2 cup unsalted butter, melted
- 2 large eggs
- Non-stick cooking spray or additional butter for greasing the waffle iron

For Serving:

- Maple syrup or honey
- Butter (optional)

Instructions:

1. Prepare the Fried Chicken:

    In a shallow dish, mix together the flour, salt, black pepper, paprika, and garlic powder.

Dip each chicken breast into the beaten eggs, then dredge in the flour mixture, coating evenly.

Heat vegetable oil in a large skillet over medium-high heat. Fry the chicken breasts until golden brown and cooked through, about 5-7 minutes per side.

Transfer to a paper towel-lined plate to drain excess oil.

2. Prepare the Waffles:

Preheat your waffle iron according to the manufacturer's instructions.

In a large mixing bowl, whisk together the flour, sugar, baking powder, and salt.

In another bowl, whisk together the milk, melted butter, and eggs.

Pour the wet ingredients into the dry ingredients and stir until just combined. Do not overmix; a few lumps are okay.

Lightly grease the waffle iron with non-stick cooking spray or brush with melted butter.

Pour the batter onto the preheated waffle iron and cook according to the manufacturer's instructions until golden brown and crisp.

Repeat with the remaining batter.

3. Assemble Chicken and Waffles:

Place one or two waffles on a plate.

Top each waffle with a fried chicken breast.

Drizzle with maple syrup or honey.

Optionally, add a pat of butter on top of the chicken.

Serve immediately and enjoy the sweet and savory combination of chicken and waffles!

Feel free to customize your chicken and waffles by adding hot sauce, gravy, or other toppings according to your preference. Enjoy this indulgent dish for breakfast, brunch, or even dinner!

**BLT sandwich**

Ingredients:

- 8 slices of bread (toasted, if desired)
- 8 slices of bacon
- 4 leaves of lettuce (Romaine or iceberg work well)
- 2 ripe tomatoes, sliced
- Mayonnaise
- Salt and pepper, to taste

Instructions:

Cook the bacon in a skillet over medium heat until crispy. Transfer to a paper towel-lined plate to drain excess grease.
If desired, toast the bread slices until golden brown.
Spread a thin layer of mayonnaise on one side of each slice of bread.
Arrange the lettuce leaves on 4 slices of bread.
Top the lettuce with slices of tomato.
Season the tomato slices with salt and pepper, to taste.
Place 2 slices of crispy bacon on top of each tomato layer.
Place the remaining 4 slices of bread on top to complete the sandwiches, mayonnaise side down.
Use a sharp knife to slice each sandwich diagonally into halves.
Serve the BLT sandwiches immediately, and enjoy!

Feel free to customize your BLT sandwich by adding avocado slices, a fried egg, or your favorite condiments. Serve it with a side of chips, coleslaw, or a crisp pickle for a delicious and satisfying meal.

**Corned beef hash**

Ingredients:

- 2 cups cooked corned beef, diced
- 2 cups potatoes, peeled and diced
- 1 small onion, diced
- 2 tablespoons butter or vegetable oil
- Salt and pepper, to taste
- Optional seasonings: paprika, garlic powder, thyme, etc.
- Chopped fresh parsley, for garnish (optional)
- Fried or poached eggs, for serving (optional)

Instructions:

1. Cook Potatoes:

   Place the diced potatoes in a pot of salted water and bring to a boil.
   Reduce heat to medium-low and simmer until the potatoes are tender, about 10-15 minutes.
   Drain the potatoes and set aside.

2. Cook Corned Beef Hash:

   Heat butter or vegetable oil in a large skillet over medium heat.
   Add diced onions to the skillet and cook until softened and translucent, about 3-4 minutes.
   Add the diced corned beef and cooked potatoes to the skillet, spreading them out in an even layer.
   Season with salt, pepper, and any optional seasonings to taste.
   Allow the mixture to cook without stirring for a few minutes to develop a crispy crust on the bottom.
   Use a spatula to flip sections of the hash, allowing the other side to brown as well. Repeat this process until the hash is golden brown and crispy on all sides, about 10-12 minutes.
   Taste and adjust seasoning if necessary.

3. Serve:

    Once the corned beef hash is crispy and golden brown, remove it from the heat.
    Transfer the hash to a serving platter or individual plates.
    Garnish with chopped fresh parsley if desired.
    Serve hot, optionally topped with fried or poached eggs.

Enjoy your homemade corned beef hash for breakfast, brunch, or any meal of the day! It pairs well with toast, biscuits, or a side of fruit.

**Monte Cristo sandwich**

Ingredients:

For the Sandwich:

- 8 slices of bread (white or whole wheat)
- 8 slices of ham
- 8 slices of Swiss cheese
- Dijon mustard (optional)
- Butter, softened

For the Egg Batter:

- 2 large eggs
- 1/4 cup milk
- 1/4 teaspoon salt
- 1/4 teaspoon black pepper

For Frying:

- Butter or oil for frying

For Serving:

- Powdered sugar
- Jam or preserves (optional)

Instructions:

1. Assemble the Sandwiches:

    Lay out 8 slices of bread on a clean surface.
    Spread a thin layer of Dijon mustard on each slice of bread (optional).
    Layer each slice of bread with a slice of Swiss cheese and a slice of ham.
    Place another slice of bread on top to complete the sandwiches.

2. Prepare the Egg Batter:

   In a shallow dish or bowl, whisk together the eggs, milk, salt, and black pepper until well combined.

3. Dip and Coat:

   Dip each assembled sandwich into the egg batter, ensuring both sides are coated.
   Allow any excess batter to drip off.

4. Fry the Sandwiches:

   Heat a large skillet or griddle over medium heat and add butter or oil.
   Place the dipped sandwiches in the skillet and cook until golden brown on one side, about 3-4 minutes.
   Flip the sandwiches and cook until golden brown on the other side and the cheese is melted, about 3-4 minutes more.
   Repeat with the remaining sandwiches, adding more butter or oil to the skillet as needed.

5. Serve:

   Remove the Monte Cristo sandwiches from the skillet and transfer to a serving plate.
   Dust the sandwiches with powdered sugar.
   Serve hot with jam or preserves on the side for dipping, if desired.

Enjoy the delicious combination of savory ham and cheese with the sweet and crispy exterior of the Monte Cristo sandwich!

**Denver omelette**

Ingredients:

- 3 large eggs
- 1/4 cup diced cooked ham
- 1/4 cup diced bell peppers (any color)
- 1/4 cup diced onion
- 1/4 cup shredded cheddar cheese
- Salt and pepper, to taste
- 1 tablespoon butter or oil for cooking
- Optional toppings: diced tomatoes, sliced avocado, salsa, sour cream

Instructions:

1. Prepare Ingredients:

    In a small bowl, beat the eggs until well combined. Season with salt and pepper to taste. Set aside.
    Dice the ham, bell peppers, and onion.

2. Cook Filling:

    Heat butter or oil in a non-stick skillet over medium heat.
    Add the diced ham, bell peppers, and onion to the skillet. Cook, stirring occasionally, until the vegetables are tender and the ham is heated through, about 3-4 minutes.

3. Make Omelette:

    Pour the beaten eggs into the skillet with the cooked ham and vegetables.
    Allow the eggs to set slightly around the edges, then use a spatula to gently push the cooked portions toward the center, tilting the skillet to let the uncooked eggs flow to the edges.
    Continue cooking until the eggs are mostly set but still slightly runny on top.

4. Add Cheese:

Sprinkle the shredded cheddar cheese evenly over one half of the omelette.
Allow the cheese to melt slightly.

5. Fold and Serve:

   Using a spatula, carefully fold the unfilled half of the omelette over the cheese-covered half to form a half-moon shape.
   Cook for another minute to ensure the cheese is fully melted and the omelette is heated through.

6. Serve:

   Slide the Denver omelette onto a serving plate.
   Garnish with optional toppings such as diced tomatoes, sliced avocado, salsa, or sour cream, if desired.
   Serve hot and enjoy!

This Denver omelette is a hearty and satisfying breakfast option that's packed with flavor and perfect for starting your day off right.

**Philly cheesesteak**

Ingredients:

- 1 pound (450g) ribeye steak, thinly sliced (you can also use sirloin or top round)
- 2 tablespoons vegetable oil or olive oil
- 1 large onion, thinly sliced
- 1 large green bell pepper, thinly sliced (optional)
- Salt and pepper, to taste
- 4 to 6 slices of provolone cheese (or Cheese Whiz for a traditional Philly cheesesteak)
- 4 hoagie rolls or sub rolls

Instructions:

1. Prepare the Steak:

   If the steak is not already thinly sliced, place it in the freezer for about 30 minutes to firm up, which makes it easier to slice thinly.
   Once firm, thinly slice the steak against the grain. Set aside.

2. Sauté the Onions and Peppers:

   Heat 1 tablespoon of oil in a large skillet over medium-high heat.
   Add the sliced onions and bell peppers (if using) to the skillet. Sauté until softened and caramelized, about 5-7 minutes. Remove from skillet and set aside.

3. Cook the Steak:

   In the same skillet, heat the remaining tablespoon of oil over medium-high heat.
   Add the sliced steak to the skillet in an even layer. Season with salt and pepper to taste.
   Cook the steak, stirring occasionally, until browned and cooked through, about 3-4 minutes.

4. Assemble the Cheesesteaks:

   Preheat your oven broiler.
   Split the hoagie rolls and place them on a baking sheet.
   Divide the cooked steak evenly among the hoagie rolls.

Top each pile of steak with a portion of the sautéed onions and peppers.
Place 1 to 1 1/2 slices of provolone cheese on top of each sandwich.

5. Broil the Cheesesteaks:

    Place the baking sheet under the broiler and broil until the cheese is melted and bubbly, about 1-2 minutes. Watch closely to prevent burning.

6. Serve:

    Remove the Philly cheesesteaks from the oven.
    Close the hoagie rolls and serve immediately while warm.

Enjoy your homemade Philly cheesesteaks with your favorite sides such as fries, chips, or a crisp salad.

**Biscuits and gravy**

Ingredients:

For the Biscuits:

- 2 cups all-purpose flour
- 1 tablespoon baking powder
- 1 teaspoon sugar
- 1/2 teaspoon salt
- 1/2 cup unsalted butter, cold and cubed
- 3/4 cup milk

For the Sausage Gravy:

- 1/2 lb (225g) breakfast sausage (pork or turkey)
- 2 tablespoons all-purpose flour
- 2 cups milk
- Salt and pepper, to taste
- Optional: red pepper flakes, paprika, sage, thyme for additional flavor

Instructions:

1. Prepare the Biscuits:

    Preheat your oven to 425°F (220°C).
    In a large mixing bowl, whisk together the flour, baking powder, sugar, and salt.
    Cut in the cold cubed butter using a pastry cutter or two knives until the mixture resembles coarse crumbs.
    Gradually add the milk, stirring until the dough comes together.
    Turn the dough out onto a floured surface and knead gently until it comes together.
    Roll out the dough to about 1/2-inch thickness.
    Use a biscuit cutter or a glass to cut out biscuits. Place them on a baking sheet lined with parchment paper.
    Gather any scraps of dough, reroll, and cut out additional biscuits.
    Bake the biscuits in the preheated oven for 12-15 minutes, or until golden brown.

2. Prepare the Sausage Gravy:

While the biscuits are baking, cook the breakfast sausage in a large skillet over medium heat. Use a spatula to break the sausage into smaller pieces as it cooks. Once the sausage is fully cooked and browned, sprinkle the flour over the sausage, stirring to combine. Cook for 1-2 minutes to allow the flour to cook off any raw taste.
Gradually pour in the milk, stirring constantly to prevent lumps from forming. Continue cooking the gravy, stirring frequently, until it thickens to your desired consistency, about 5-7 minutes.
Season the gravy with salt, pepper, and any additional spices or herbs to taste.

3. Serve:

Split the warm biscuits in half and place them on serving plates.
Ladle the hot sausage gravy over the biscuits.
Serve immediately and enjoy!

Biscuits and gravy is perfect for breakfast or brunch and is sure to warm you up on a cold morning.

**Tuna melt sandwich**

Ingredients:

For the Tuna Salad:

- 2 cans (5 ounces each) of tuna, drained
- 1/4 cup mayonnaise
- 2 tablespoons chopped celery
- 2 tablespoons chopped red onion
- 1 tablespoon chopped fresh parsley (optional)
- 1 tablespoon lemon juice
- Salt and pepper, to taste

For the Sandwich:

- 4 slices of bread (white, whole wheat, or your choice)
- Butter or mayonnaise for spreading
- 4 slices of cheese (cheddar, Swiss, provolone, or your choice)
- Optional toppings: sliced tomato, avocado, lettuce, etc.

Instructions:

1. Prepare the Tuna Salad:

    In a mixing bowl, combine the drained tuna, mayonnaise, chopped celery, chopped red onion, chopped parsley (if using), and lemon juice.
    Season with salt and pepper to taste. Mix until well combined. Adjust seasoning if needed.

2. Assemble the Sandwich:

    Preheat your oven broiler or a toaster oven.
    Spread butter or mayonnaise on one side of each slice of bread.
    Place the bread slices, buttered side down, on a baking sheet lined with parchment paper.

Divide the prepared tuna salad evenly among two slices of bread, spreading it out to cover the entire slice.
Top each tuna-covered slice of bread with a slice of cheese.
Add any optional toppings, such as sliced tomato or avocado, if desired.
Place the remaining two slices of bread on top of each sandwich to complete them.

3. Toast the Sandwich:

Place the baking sheet with assembled sandwiches under the preheated broiler or in the toaster oven.
Toast the sandwiches until the cheese is melted and bubbly, and the bread is golden brown, about 3-5 minutes. Watch closely to prevent burning.

4. Serve:

Remove the tuna melt sandwiches from the oven.
Carefully transfer them to serving plates.
Serve hot and enjoy!

Tuna melt sandwiches are perfect for lunch or dinner and can be customized with your favorite toppings and cheese. They're quick and easy to make and are sure to satisfy your craving for a warm and cheesy meal.

**Eggs Benedict**

Ingredients:

For the Hollandaise Sauce:

- 3 egg yolks
- 1 tablespoon lemon juice
- 1/2 cup unsalted butter, melted
- Pinch of cayenne pepper
- Salt, to taste

For the Eggs Benedict:

- 4 large eggs
- 4 slices Canadian bacon or ham
- 2 English muffins, split and toasted
- Chopped fresh parsley or chives, for garnish (optional)
- Salt and pepper, to taste

Instructions:

1. Prepare the Hollandaise Sauce:

    Fill a saucepan with a few inches of water and bring it to a gentle simmer over medium heat.
    In a heatproof bowl that fits snugly over the saucepan, whisk together the egg yolks and lemon juice until well combined.
    Place the bowl over the simmering water (make sure the bottom of the bowl doesn't touch the water).
    Gradually whisk in the melted butter, a little at a time, until the sauce thickens and becomes smooth and creamy.
    Remove the bowl from the heat and stir in the cayenne pepper and salt to taste.
    Keep warm while you prepare the rest of the dish, stirring occasionally.

2. Poach the Eggs:

Fill a large saucepan or deep skillet with about 2-3 inches of water and bring it to a gentle simmer over medium heat.

Crack each egg into a small bowl or ramekin.

Using a spoon, create a gentle whirlpool in the simmering water.

Carefully slide each egg into the whirlpool, one at a time. Cook for 3-4 minutes for a soft yolk, or longer if you prefer a firmer yolk.

Use a slotted spoon to carefully remove the poached eggs from the water and transfer them to a plate lined with paper towels to drain.

3. Assemble the Eggs Benedict:

While the eggs are poaching, place the Canadian bacon or ham slices in a dry skillet over medium heat. Cook until heated through and slightly browned, about 2-3 minutes per side.

Place the toasted English muffin halves on serving plates.

Top each English muffin half with a slice of Canadian bacon or ham.

Carefully place a poached egg on top of each slice of Canadian bacon or ham.

Spoon hollandaise sauce generously over each poached egg.

Garnish with chopped fresh parsley or chives, if desired. Season with salt and pepper to taste.

4. Serve:

Serve the Eggs Benedict immediately, while still warm.

Enjoy your delicious homemade Eggs Benedict for breakfast or brunch!

Eggs Benedict is a classic and elegant dish that is sure to impress your family and friends. It's perfect for special occasions or leisurely weekend brunches.

**Patty melt**

Ingredients:

For the Patty:

- 1/2 lb (225g) ground beef
- Salt and pepper, to taste
- 1 tablespoon vegetable oil or butter

For the Sandwich:

- 2 slices of rye bread (or your preferred bread)
- 2 slices of Swiss cheese
- 1/4 cup caramelized onions (optional)
- Butter, softened

Instructions:

1. Prepare the Patty:

   Divide the ground beef into two equal portions and shape them into patties.
   Season both sides of each patty with salt and pepper.
   Heat vegetable oil or butter in a skillet over medium-high heat.
   Cook the patties for 3-4 minutes on each side, or until they reach your desired level of doneness. Remove from the skillet and set aside.

2. Assemble the Sandwich:

   Spread softened butter on one side of each slice of rye bread.
   Place one slice of bread, butter side down, on a clean surface or in the skillet.
   Place a slice of Swiss cheese on top of the bread.
   Place one cooked beef patty on top of the cheese.
   Add a layer of caramelized onions on top of the beef patty, if using.
   Place the second slice of bread on top, butter side up.

3. Grill the Sandwich:

Heat a skillet or griddle over medium heat.
Place the assembled sandwich in the skillet or on the griddle.
Cook for 3-4 minutes on each side, or until the bread is toasted and the cheese is melted.
Press down on the sandwich gently with a spatula while cooking to help the ingredients meld together.

4. Serve:

Remove the patty melt from the skillet or griddle and transfer it to a cutting board.
Use a sharp knife to slice the sandwich in half diagonally.
Serve hot and enjoy your delicious homemade patty melt!

Patty melts are a comforting and flavorful meal that's perfect for lunch or dinner. Serve them with your favorite side dishes such as fries, coleslaw, or a crisp salad for a complete meal.

**Western omelette**

Ingredients:

- 3 large eggs
- 2 tablespoons milk
- Salt and pepper, to taste
- 1/4 cup diced ham
- 1/4 cup diced bell peppers (any color)
- 1/4 cup diced onion
- 1/4 cup shredded cheddar cheese
- 1 tablespoon butter or oil for cooking
- Optional toppings: salsa, sour cream, avocado slices

Instructions:

1. Prepare Ingredients:

    In a small bowl, whisk together the eggs, milk, salt, and pepper until well combined. Set aside.
    Dice the ham, bell peppers, and onion.

2. Cook Filling:

    Heat butter or oil in a non-stick skillet over medium heat.
    Add the diced ham, bell peppers, and onion to the skillet. Sauté until softened, about 3-4 minutes. Remove from skillet and set aside.

3. Make Omelette:

    Wipe out the skillet if necessary and return it to the stove over medium heat.
    Pour the egg mixture into the skillet. As the eggs begin to set, use a spatula to gently push the cooked portions toward the center, tilting the skillet to let the uncooked eggs flow to the edges.
    Continue cooking until the eggs are mostly set but still slightly runny on top.

4. Add Fillings:

Sprinkle the shredded cheddar cheese evenly over one half of the omelette.
Spoon the cooked ham, bell peppers, and onion mixture on top of the cheese.

5. Fold and Serve:

    Carefully fold the unfilled half of the omelette over the filled half to form a half-moon shape.
    Cook for another minute to allow the cheese to melt and the omelette to heat through.

6. Serve:

    Slide the Western omelette onto a serving plate.
    Garnish with optional toppings such as salsa, sour cream, or avocado slices, if desired.
    Serve hot and enjoy your delicious Western omelette!

This hearty and flavorful breakfast dish is perfect for starting your day off right. You can also customize it with your favorite fillings and toppings to suit your taste preferences.

**Meatloaf with mashed potatoes**

Ingredients:

For the Meatloaf:

- 1 1/2 pounds (680g) ground beef (you can also use a mix of ground beef and ground pork)
- 1 cup breadcrumbs
- 1/2 cup milk
- 1/2 cup finely chopped onion
- 1/4 cup finely chopped bell pepper (optional)
- 2 cloves garlic, minced
- 2 eggs, beaten
- 2 tablespoons Worcestershire sauce
- 1 tablespoon Dijon mustard
- 1 teaspoon salt
- 1/2 teaspoon black pepper
- 1/4 cup ketchup or BBQ sauce

For the Mashed Potatoes:

- 2 pounds (about 900g) potatoes (russet or Yukon Gold), peeled and cut into chunks
- 1/2 cup milk
- 4 tablespoons butter
- Salt and pepper, to taste
- Chopped fresh parsley or chives for garnish (optional)

Instructions:

1. Preheat Oven and Prepare Meatloaf:

    Preheat your oven to 350°F (175°C).
    In a large mixing bowl, combine the ground beef, breadcrumbs, milk, chopped onion, bell pepper (if using), minced garlic, beaten eggs, Worcestershire sauce, Dijon mustard, salt, and black pepper. Mix until well combined.
    Transfer the meatloaf mixture to a 9x5-inch loaf pan, shaping it into a loaf shape.
    Spread the ketchup or BBQ sauce evenly over the top of the meatloaf.

2. Bake the Meatloaf:

    Place the meatloaf in the preheated oven and bake for 60-75 minutes, or until the meatloaf is cooked through and the top is browned.
    Remove from the oven and let it rest for a few minutes before slicing.

3. Prepare Mashed Potatoes:

    While the meatloaf is baking, place the potato chunks in a large pot and cover with cold water. Add a generous pinch of salt.
    Bring the water to a boil, then reduce heat to medium-low and simmer until the potatoes are fork-tender, about 15-20 minutes.
    Drain the potatoes and return them to the pot.
    Add the milk and butter to the pot with the potatoes.
    Mash the potatoes with a potato masher until smooth and creamy. Season with salt and pepper to taste.

4. Serve:

    Slice the meatloaf and serve it with a generous portion of mashed potatoes.
    Garnish with chopped fresh parsley or chives, if desired.
    Enjoy your comforting and delicious meatloaf with mashed potatoes!

Feel free to serve the meatloaf with your favorite gravy or additional toppings, and add some steamed vegetables or a side salad to complete the meal.

**Grilled cheese sandwich**

Ingredients:

- 2 slices of bread (any type you prefer, such as white, whole wheat, sourdough, etc.)
- 2 slices of cheese (cheddar, American, Swiss, or your favorite cheese)
- Butter or margarine, softened

Instructions:

1. Assemble the Sandwich:

    Place one slice of cheese on one slice of bread.
    Place the second slice of cheese on the other slice of bread.
    Put the two slices of bread together to form a sandwich, with the cheese slices in the middle.

2. Butter the Bread:

    Spread softened butter or margarine evenly over one side of the sandwich.
    This buttered side will be placed facing down on the skillet or griddle.

3. Heat the Skillet or Griddle:

    Heat a skillet or griddle over medium heat.
    Make sure the surface is hot before placing the sandwich on it.

4. Cook the Sandwich:

    Place the sandwich, buttered side down, on the skillet or griddle.
    Cook for 2-3 minutes, or until the bottom side is golden brown and crispy.
    While the first side is cooking, spread butter on the top side of the sandwich.
    Use a spatula to carefully flip the sandwich over.
    Cook for an additional 2-3 minutes, or until the second side is golden brown and crispy, and the cheese is melted.

5. Serve:

    Remove the grilled cheese sandwich from the skillet or griddle and place it on a cutting board.
    Allow it to cool for a minute or two before slicing, to avoid burning your mouth.
    Slice the sandwich diagonally, if desired, and serve hot.

Optional Additions:

- You can customize your grilled cheese sandwich by adding ingredients such as sliced tomatoes, cooked bacon, ham, avocado slices, caramelized onions, or fresh herbs.
- You can also experiment with different types of bread and cheese to create unique flavor combinations.

Enjoy your homemade grilled cheese sandwich as a quick and comforting meal, perfect for lunch or dinner!

**Huevos Rancheros**

Ingredients:

For the Ranchero Sauce:

- 1 tablespoon vegetable oil
- 1/2 onion, finely chopped
- 2 cloves garlic, minced
- 1 jalapeño or serrano pepper, seeded and minced (optional, for heat)
- 1 can (14.5 ounces) diced tomatoes
- 1 teaspoon ground cumin
- 1 teaspoon chili powder
- Salt and pepper, to taste

For the Huevos Rancheros:

- 4 corn tortillas
- Vegetable oil, for frying
- 4 eggs
- Salt and pepper, to taste
- 1/2 cup refried beans (optional)
- 1/2 cup shredded cheese (cheddar, Monterey Jack, or queso fresco)
- Chopped fresh cilantro, for garnish
- Sliced avocado, for garnish
- Lime wedges, for serving

Instructions:

1. Prepare the Ranchero Sauce:

    Heat vegetable oil in a skillet over medium heat.
    Add the chopped onion and cook until softened, about 3-4 minutes.
    Add the minced garlic and jalapeño or serrano pepper (if using) and cook for another minute.
    Stir in the diced tomatoes (with their juices), ground cumin, chili powder, salt, and pepper.

Simmer the sauce for about 10-15 minutes, until it thickens slightly. Taste and adjust seasoning as needed. Remove from heat and set aside.

2. Prepare the Tortillas:

In another skillet, heat a small amount of vegetable oil over medium-high heat. Lightly fry the corn tortillas one at a time until they are just starting to crisp up, about 1-2 minutes per side. Drain on paper towels and set aside.

3. Fry the Eggs:

In the same skillet used for frying the tortillas, fry the eggs to your desired doneness (sunny-side-up or over-easy).
Season the eggs with salt and pepper while cooking.

4. Assemble the Huevos Rancheros:

Spread a thin layer of refried beans (if using) on each fried tortilla.
Place a fried egg on top of each tortilla.
Spoon the Ranchero sauce over the eggs and tortillas.
Sprinkle shredded cheese over the top.
Garnish with chopped fresh cilantro and sliced avocado.

5. Serve:

Serve the Huevos Rancheros immediately, with lime wedges on the side for squeezing over the top.
Enjoy your delicious and satisfying Huevos Rancheros for breakfast or brunch!

Feel free to customize your Huevos Rancheros by adding other toppings such as sliced radishes, diced onions, or hot sauce according to your taste preferences.

**Turkey club sandwich**

Ingredients:

- 3 slices of bread (white, whole wheat, or your choice)
- 3-4 slices of roasted turkey breast
- 2-3 slices of cooked bacon
- 1-2 leaves of lettuce (such as iceberg or romaine)
- 2 slices of tomato
- Mayonnaise
- Salt and pepper, to taste
- Toothpicks (optional, for securing the sandwich)

Instructions:

1. Toast the Bread:

    Toast the slices of bread until golden brown and crispy. You can use a toaster or a skillet for toasting.

2. Prepare the Ingredients:

    Cook the bacon until crispy, then drain on paper towels.
    Slice the tomato into thin slices.
    Wash and dry the lettuce leaves.

3. Assemble the Sandwich:

    Spread a thin layer of mayonnaise on one side of each slice of bread.
    Place a leaf of lettuce on one slice of bread.
    Layer the sliced turkey on top of the lettuce.
    Season the turkey with a pinch of salt and pepper.
    Place the second slice of bread on top of the turkey.
    Layer the cooked bacon slices on top of the second slice of bread.
    Place the sliced tomato on top of the bacon.
    Add another leaf of lettuce on top of the tomato.

Spread mayonnaise on one side of the third slice of bread, then place it on top of the sandwich, mayonnaise side down.

4. Cut and Serve:

Use a sharp knife to cut the sandwich diagonally into two halves or quarters.
If desired, secure the sandwich layers with toothpicks to hold everything together.
Serve immediately and enjoy your delicious turkey club sandwich!

Feel free to customize your turkey club sandwich by adding avocado slices, cheese, or any other favorite toppings you prefer. Serve it with a side of potato chips, coleslaw, or a crisp pickle for a classic lunchtime meal.

**Chicken fried steak with gravy**

Ingredients:

For the Chicken Fried Steak:

- 4 cube steaks (tenderized round or sirloin steak)
- 1 cup all-purpose flour
- 1 teaspoon salt
- 1/2 teaspoon black pepper
- 1/2 teaspoon garlic powder
- 1/2 teaspoon paprika
- 2 large eggs
- 1/4 cup milk
- Vegetable oil, for frying

For the Gravy:

- 1/4 cup pan drippings (from frying the steaks)
- 1/4 cup all-purpose flour
- 2 cups beef broth (or chicken broth)
- Salt and pepper, to taste

Instructions:

1. Prepare the Steaks:

    In a shallow dish, combine the flour, salt, black pepper, garlic powder, and paprika.
    In another shallow dish, whisk together the eggs and milk.
    Dredge each cube steak in the flour mixture, shaking off any excess.
    Dip the floured steak into the egg mixture, then dredge it again in the flour mixture, pressing gently to adhere. Repeat with the remaining steaks.

2. Fry the Steaks:

Heat vegetable oil in a large skillet over medium-high heat until hot but not smoking.

Carefully add the breaded steaks to the skillet, being careful not to overcrowd the pan. You may need to fry the steaks in batches.

Cook the steaks for 3-4 minutes per side, or until golden brown and cooked through.

Remove the cooked steaks from the skillet and transfer them to a plate lined with paper towels to drain excess oil. Keep warm while you make the gravy.

3. Make the Gravy:

Drain all but about 1/4 cup of the pan drippings from the skillet, reserving them for the gravy.

Place the skillet back over medium heat. Sprinkle the flour evenly over the pan drippings.

Cook the flour, stirring constantly, until it becomes golden brown and fragrant, about 2-3 minutes.

Gradually pour in the beef broth (or chicken broth), whisking constantly to prevent lumps from forming.

Continue cooking and whisking until the gravy thickens to your desired consistency, about 5-7 minutes.

Season the gravy with salt and pepper to taste.

4. Serve:

Spoon the gravy over the chicken fried steaks.

Serve hot, alongside mashed potatoes, green beans, or your favorite sides.

Enjoy your homemade chicken fried steak with gravy, a comforting and hearty dish that's sure to satisfy!

**Chili cheese fries**

Ingredients:

For the Chili:

- 1 tablespoon olive oil
- 1 small onion, diced
- 2 cloves garlic, minced
- 1 pound (450g) ground beef
- 1 can (14.5 ounces) diced tomatoes
- 1 can (15 ounces) kidney beans, drained and rinsed
- 2 tablespoons tomato paste
- 1 tablespoon chili powder
- 1 teaspoon ground cumin
- 1/2 teaspoon paprika
- Salt and pepper, to taste

For the Cheese Sauce:

- 2 tablespoons butter
- 2 tablespoons all-purpose flour
- 1 cup milk
- 1 cup shredded cheddar cheese
- Salt and pepper, to taste

For the Fries:

- 1 pound (450g) frozen french fries
- Salt, to taste

Optional Toppings:

- Sliced jalapeños
- Chopped green onions
- Sour cream
- Guacamole

- Salsa

Instructions:

1. Prepare the Chili:

   Heat olive oil in a large skillet over medium heat.
   Add diced onion and minced garlic to the skillet. Cook until softened, about 2-3 minutes.
   Add ground beef to the skillet. Cook until browned and no longer pink, breaking it up with a spoon as it cooks.
   Stir in diced tomatoes, kidney beans, tomato paste, chili powder, cumin, paprika, salt, and pepper. Bring to a simmer and cook for 10-15 minutes, stirring occasionally, until flavors are well combined and chili has thickened slightly. Remove from heat and set aside.

2. Prepare the Cheese Sauce:

   In a saucepan, melt butter over medium heat.
   Whisk in flour to form a roux. Cook for 1-2 minutes, stirring constantly.
   Gradually pour in milk, whisking constantly to prevent lumps from forming. Continue cooking and whisking until the mixture thickens, about 3-4 minutes.
   Stir in shredded cheddar cheese until melted and smooth. Season with salt and pepper to taste. Remove from heat and set aside.

3. Cook the Fries:

   Preheat oven according to the package instructions for the frozen french fries.
   Spread the frozen french fries in a single layer on a baking sheet.
   Bake according to the package instructions until golden brown and crispy.
   Season the cooked fries with salt to taste.

4. Assemble the Chili Cheese Fries:

   Arrange the cooked french fries on a serving platter or individual plates.
   Spoon the chili over the fries.
   Drizzle the cheese sauce over the chili.

Optional: Top with sliced jalapeños, chopped green onions, sour cream, guacamole, or salsa.

5. Serve:

Serve the chili cheese fries immediately while hot and enjoy!

Chili cheese fries make a fantastic appetizer, snack, or indulgent meal that's perfect for sharing with friends and family.

**Breakfast burrito**

Ingredients:

- 4 large eggs
- Salt and pepper, to taste
- 4 large flour tortillas
- 4 slices of bacon or sausage links, cooked and crumbled
- 1/2 cup shredded cheese (cheddar, Monterey Jack, or your favorite)
- Optional fillings: diced cooked potatoes, sautéed bell peppers and onions, chopped tomatoes, avocado slices, salsa, sour cream, chopped cilantro

Instructions:

1. Prepare the Eggs:

   Crack the eggs into a bowl and whisk until well beaten.
   Season with salt and pepper to taste.
   Heat a non-stick skillet over medium heat.
   Pour the beaten eggs into the skillet and cook, stirring occasionally, until scrambled and cooked through. Remove from heat.

2. Assemble the Burritos:

   Warm the flour tortillas in the microwave for a few seconds or in a dry skillet over medium heat for about 30 seconds on each side to make them pliable.
   Divide the scrambled eggs evenly among the tortillas, placing them in the center.
   Sprinkle the crumbled bacon or sausage over the eggs.
   Add any additional fillings of your choice, such as shredded cheese, diced cooked potatoes, sautéed bell peppers and onions, chopped tomatoes, avocado slices, salsa, sour cream, or chopped cilantro.

3. Roll the Burritos:

   Fold the sides of the tortilla over the filling.
   Fold the bottom edge of the tortilla over the filling, then roll it up tightly to form a burrito.

4. Serve:

> Serve the breakfast burritos immediately, or wrap them in aluminum foil to keep them warm until ready to serve.
> You can also cut them in half diagonally for easier handling.

Enjoy your homemade breakfast burritos as a delicious and satisfying meal to start your day off right! Feel free to customize the fillings to suit your taste preferences. They're perfect for breakfast on the go or a leisurely weekend brunch.

**Fish and chips**

Ingredients:

For the Fish:

- 4 fillets of white fish (such as cod, haddock, or pollock)
- 1 cup all-purpose flour
- 1 teaspoon baking powder
- 1 teaspoon salt
- 1/2 teaspoon black pepper
- 1 cup cold beer (lager or ale)
- Vegetable oil, for frying

For the Chips:

- 4 large potatoes, peeled and cut into thick fries
- Vegetable oil, for frying
- Salt, to taste

Instructions:

1. Prepare the Fish:

   In a mixing bowl, whisk together the flour, baking powder, salt, and black pepper. Gradually pour in the cold beer, whisking until the batter is smooth and well combined.
   Cover the bowl with plastic wrap and let the batter rest in the refrigerator for 30 minutes.

2. Prepare the Chips:

   Rinse the cut potatoes under cold water to remove excess starch.
   Pat the potatoes dry with paper towels.
   Heat vegetable oil in a deep fryer or large pot to 325°F (165°C).
   Carefully add the potato fries to the hot oil, working in batches if necessary to avoid overcrowding the fryer.
   Fry the potatoes for 4-5 minutes, or until they are partially cooked but still pale in color.
   Remove the partially cooked fries from the oil and drain them on paper towels.

Increase the temperature of the oil to 375°F (190°C).
Return the partially cooked fries to the hot oil and fry them again for 3-4 minutes, or until they are golden brown and crispy.
Remove the fries from the oil and drain them on fresh paper towels. Season with salt to taste.

3. Fry the Fish:

   Heat vegetable oil in a deep fryer or large pot to 375°F (190°C).
   Dip each fish fillet into the batter, allowing any excess batter to drip off.
   Carefully place the battered fish fillets into the hot oil, working in batches if necessary to avoid overcrowding the fryer.
   Fry the fish for 4-5 minutes, or until they are golden brown and cooked through.
   Remove the fried fish from the oil and drain them on paper towels.

4. Serve:

   Serve the fish and chips hot, with tartar sauce, malt vinegar, or lemon wedges on the side for dipping.
   Enjoy your homemade fish and chips as a delicious and satisfying meal!

Fish and chips are best enjoyed fresh and hot, straight from the fryer. They're a classic comfort food that's perfect for a casual dinner or a fun meal with friends and family.

**Fried chicken and biscuits**

Ingredients:

For the Fried Chicken:

- 4 bone-in, skin-on chicken thighs or breasts
- 1 cup buttermilk
- 1 teaspoon salt
- 1/2 teaspoon black pepper
- 1/2 teaspoon paprika
- 1/4 teaspoon garlic powder
- 1/4 teaspoon onion powder
- 1/4 teaspoon cayenne pepper (optional)
- 1 cup all-purpose flour
- Vegetable oil, for frying

For the Biscuits:

- 2 cups all-purpose flour
- 1 tablespoon baking powder
- 1 teaspoon salt
- 1/2 cup unsalted butter, cold and cubed
- 3/4 cup milk

Instructions:

1. Prepare the Fried Chicken:

> In a bowl, combine the buttermilk, salt, black pepper, paprika, garlic powder, onion powder, and cayenne pepper (if using). Mix well.
> Place the chicken pieces in the buttermilk mixture, ensuring they are fully coated.
> Cover the bowl and refrigerate for at least 1 hour, or overnight for best results.
> In a shallow dish, combine the flour with additional salt and pepper to taste.
> Remove the chicken from the buttermilk mixture, allowing any excess to drip off.
> Dredge the chicken pieces in the seasoned flour mixture, shaking off any excess.
> Heat vegetable oil in a large skillet or Dutch oven over medium-high heat until it reaches 350°F (175°C).
> Carefully place the coated chicken pieces in the hot oil, working in batches if necessary to avoid overcrowding the pan.

Fry the chicken for 6-8 minutes per side, or until golden brown and cooked through (internal temperature should reach 165°F or 75°C).

Transfer the fried chicken to a wire rack set over a baking sheet to drain excess oil. Keep warm while you prepare the biscuits.

2. Prepare the Biscuits:

   Preheat your oven to 425°F (220°C). Line a baking sheet with parchment paper.
   In a large mixing bowl, whisk together the flour, baking powder, and salt.
   Add the cold, cubed butter to the flour mixture. Use a pastry cutter or fork to cut the butter into the flour until the mixture resembles coarse crumbs.
   Pour in the milk and stir until just combined, being careful not to overmix.
   Turn the dough out onto a floured surface and gently knead it a few times until it comes together.
   Pat or roll out the dough to about 1-inch thickness. Use a biscuit cutter or the rim of a glass to cut out biscuits.
   Place the biscuits on the prepared baking sheet, leaving a little space between each one.
   Bake the biscuits in the preheated oven for 12-15 minutes, or until they are golden brown on top.

3. Serve:

   Serve the fried chicken and biscuits hot, with your favorite sides such as mashed potatoes, coleslaw, or gravy.
   Enjoy your homemade fried chicken and biscuits as a comforting and delicious meal!

This classic Southern dish is perfect for a special weekend breakfast, brunch, or dinner. Feel free to customize it with your favorite seasonings and sides to make it your own.

**Chicken pot pie**

Ingredients:

For the Pie Crust:

- 2 1/2 cups all-purpose flour
- 1 cup (2 sticks) cold unsalted butter, cut into cubes
- 1 teaspoon salt
- 1 teaspoon granulated sugar
- 1/4 to 1/2 cup ice water

For the Filling:

- 2 tablespoons unsalted butter
- 1 small onion, diced
- 2 carrots, diced
- 2 celery stalks, diced
- 2 cloves garlic, minced
- 1/4 cup all-purpose flour
- 2 cups chicken broth
- 1 cup milk or heavy cream
- 2 cups cooked chicken, diced or shredded
- 1 cup frozen peas
- Salt and pepper, to taste
- 1 teaspoon dried thyme (or 1 tablespoon fresh thyme)
- 1 egg, beaten (for egg wash)

Instructions:

1. Make the Pie Crust:

> In a large mixing bowl, combine the flour, salt, and sugar.
> Add the cold cubed butter to the flour mixture.
> Use a pastry cutter or your fingers to work the butter into the flour until the mixture resembles coarse crumbs.

Gradually add the ice water, a few tablespoons at a time, mixing with a fork until the dough just comes together. Be careful not to overwork the dough.

Divide the dough into two equal portions, shape each into a disk, wrap in plastic wrap, and refrigerate for at least 1 hour.

2. Prepare the Filling:

In a large skillet or Dutch oven, melt the butter over medium heat.

Add the diced onion, carrots, and celery to the skillet. Cook until the vegetables are softened, about 5-7 minutes.

Add the minced garlic and cook for an additional 1-2 minutes, until fragrant.

Sprinkle the flour over the vegetables and stir to coat evenly. Cook for 1-2 minutes to cook out the raw flour taste.

Gradually pour in the chicken broth and milk (or cream), stirring constantly to prevent lumps from forming.

Bring the mixture to a simmer, then cook for 5-7 minutes, or until the sauce thickens.

Stir in the cooked chicken, frozen peas, dried thyme, salt, and pepper. Remove from heat and set aside.

3. Assemble and Bake the Pie:

Preheat your oven to 400°F (200°C).

Roll out one disk of pie dough on a lightly floured surface to fit your pie dish.

Place the rolled-out dough into the bottom of the pie dish.

Pour the chicken and vegetable filling into the pie dish.

Roll out the second disk of pie dough and place it over the filling. Trim any excess dough and crimp the edges to seal.

Cut a few slits in the top crust to allow steam to escape.

Brush the top crust with beaten egg for a golden finish.

Place the pie dish on a baking sheet to catch any drips, and bake in the preheated oven for 35-40 minutes, or until the crust is golden brown and the filling is bubbling.

Remove from the oven and let it cool for a few minutes before serving.

4. Serve:

Serve the chicken pot pie hot, sliced into wedges.

Enjoy your homemade chicken pot pie as a comforting and satisfying meal!

Feel free to customize your chicken pot pie by adding other vegetables such as potatoes, mushrooms, or green beans, and adjust the seasonings to your taste preferences. It's a perfect dish for a cozy family dinner or a gathering with friends.

**Cobb salad**

Ingredients:

For the Salad:

- 6 cups mixed salad greens (such as romaine, iceberg, and arugula)
- 2 cooked chicken breasts, diced or sliced
- 8 slices bacon, cooked until crispy and chopped
- 2 hard-boiled eggs, chopped
- 1 large ripe avocado, diced
- 1 cup cherry tomatoes, halved
- 1/2 cup crumbled blue cheese or feta cheese
- 1/4 cup sliced green onions (optional)
- Salt and pepper, to taste

For the Dressing:

- 1/2 cup mayonnaise
- 2 tablespoons sour cream or Greek yogurt
- 1 tablespoon Dijon mustard
- 2 tablespoons red wine vinegar
- 1 clove garlic, minced
- Salt and pepper, to taste

Instructions:

1. Prepare the Salad:

    Arrange the mixed salad greens in a large salad bowl or on a serving platter. Arrange the diced or sliced cooked chicken breast, chopped bacon, chopped hard-boiled eggs, diced avocado, halved cherry tomatoes, crumbled blue cheese (or feta cheese), and sliced green onions (if using) in rows or sections over the salad greens.
    Season the salad with salt and pepper, to taste.

2. Prepare the Dressing:

In a small bowl, whisk together the mayonnaise, sour cream or Greek yogurt, Dijon mustard, red wine vinegar, minced garlic, salt, and pepper until smooth and well combined.

Taste and adjust the seasoning, adding more salt and pepper if needed.

3. Serve:

Drizzle the prepared dressing over the Cobb salad just before serving, or serve the dressing on the side.

Toss the salad gently to coat the ingredients with the dressing.

Serve immediately and enjoy your delicious and satisfying Cobb salad!

Cobb salad is a versatile dish, so feel free to customize it with your favorite ingredients or substitutions. You can add or omit ingredients based on your preferences or dietary restrictions. It's perfect for a light lunch or dinner and is sure to be a hit with family and friends.

**Chicken Caesar salad**

Ingredients:

For the Salad:

- 2 boneless, skinless chicken breasts
- Salt and pepper, to taste
- 1 tablespoon olive oil
- 1 head of romaine lettuce, chopped
- 1 cup croutons (store-bought or homemade)
- 1/2 cup grated Parmesan cheese
- Lemon wedges, for serving (optional)

For the Caesar Dressing:

- 1/2 cup mayonnaise
- 2 tablespoons grated Parmesan cheese
- 2 tablespoons fresh lemon juice
- 1 tablespoon Dijon mustard
- 2 cloves garlic, minced
- 1 anchovy fillet (optional), finely chopped or mashed (or 1 teaspoon anchovy paste)
- 1 teaspoon Worcestershire sauce
- Salt and pepper, to taste
- 2-3 tablespoons water (to thin out the dressing, if needed)

Instructions:

1. Prepare the Chicken:

    Season the chicken breasts with salt and pepper on both sides.
    Heat olive oil in a skillet or grill pan over medium-high heat.
    Add the seasoned chicken breasts to the skillet and cook for 6-8 minutes per side, or until they are cooked through and no longer pink in the center.
    Remove the chicken from the skillet and let it rest for a few minutes before slicing it into strips or cubes.

2. Prepare the Dressing:

> In a small bowl, whisk together the mayonnaise, grated Parmesan cheese, lemon juice, Dijon mustard, minced garlic, anchovy fillet or paste (if using), Worcestershire sauce, salt, and pepper until smooth and well combined.
> If the dressing is too thick, you can thin it out with water, a tablespoon at a time, until you reach your desired consistency. Taste and adjust the seasoning, adding more salt and pepper if needed.

3. Assemble the Salad:

> In a large salad bowl, combine the chopped romaine lettuce and sliced or cubed grilled chicken.
> Add the croutons to the salad bowl.
> Drizzle the Caesar dressing over the salad, tossing gently to coat the ingredients with the dressing.
> Sprinkle grated Parmesan cheese over the top of the salad.
> Serve the Chicken Caesar salad immediately, garnished with lemon wedges if desired.

4. Serve:

> Serve the Chicken Caesar salad as a main course for lunch or dinner.
> Enjoy your homemade Chicken Caesar salad with all the classic flavors of this beloved dish!

Feel free to customize your Chicken Caesar salad by adding additional toppings such as cherry tomatoes, sliced cucumbers, avocado slices, or bacon bits. It's a versatile and satisfying meal that's perfect for any occasion.

**Macaroni and cheese**

Ingredients:

- 8 ounces (about 2 cups) elbow macaroni or other small pasta shape
- 1/4 cup unsalted butter
- 1/4 cup all-purpose flour
- 2 cups milk (whole milk or 2% milk)
- 2 cups shredded cheese (cheddar, Monterey Jack, or a blend)
- 1/2 teaspoon salt, or to taste
- 1/4 teaspoon black pepper, or to taste
- 1/4 teaspoon paprika (optional, for garnish)
- 1/4 cup breadcrumbs (optional, for topping)

Instructions:

1. Cook the Pasta:

    Bring a large pot of salted water to a boil.
    Add the macaroni or pasta to the boiling water and cook according to the package instructions until al dente.
    Drain the cooked pasta and set aside.

2. Make the Cheese Sauce:

    In the same pot used to cook the pasta, melt the butter over medium heat.
    Once the butter is melted, whisk in the flour to form a roux. Cook the roux for 1-2 minutes, stirring constantly.
    Gradually pour in the milk while whisking constantly to prevent lumps from forming.
    Continue cooking and stirring until the sauce thickens and begins to bubble, about 5-7 minutes.
    Reduce the heat to low and stir in the shredded cheese until melted and smooth.
    Season the cheese sauce with salt and black pepper to taste.

3. Combine the Pasta and Cheese Sauce:

Add the cooked and drained pasta to the cheese sauce in the pot.
Stir until the pasta is evenly coated with the cheese sauce.
Taste and adjust seasoning, if necessary.

4. Serve:

Transfer the macaroni and cheese to a serving dish or individual bowls.
Sprinkle with paprika for color and flavor, if desired.
Optional: For a crunchy topping, sprinkle breadcrumbs over the macaroni and cheese.
Serve hot and enjoy your delicious homemade macaroni and cheese!

Macaroni and cheese can be served as a main dish or as a side dish alongside your favorite protein or vegetables. It's a comforting and satisfying meal that's loved by kids and adults alike. Feel free to customize your macaroni and cheese by adding additional ingredients such as cooked bacon, diced tomatoes, or chopped herbs.

**Vegetable omelette**

Ingredients:

- 3 large eggs
- 1/4 cup milk (optional)
- Salt and pepper, to taste
- 1 tablespoon butter or cooking oil
- 1/4 cup diced onion
- 1/4 cup diced bell pepper (any color)
- 1/4 cup diced tomato
- 1/4 cup sliced mushrooms
- 1/4 cup chopped spinach or kale (optional)
- 1/4 cup shredded cheese (cheddar, mozzarella, or your choice)
- Fresh herbs, such as parsley or chives, for garnish (optional)

Instructions:

1. Prepare the Vegetables:

    Heat a skillet over medium heat and add butter or cooking oil.
    Add diced onion, bell pepper, tomato, mushrooms, and any other vegetables you like.
    Sauté the vegetables until they are softened and slightly caramelized, about 5-7 minutes. If using spinach or kale, add it during the last minute of cooking and cook until wilted. Season with salt and pepper to taste.

2. Beat the Eggs:

    In a mixing bowl, crack the eggs and beat them with a fork or whisk until well combined.
    If desired, add milk to the beaten eggs and whisk to incorporate. This will make the omelette fluffier, but it's optional.

3. Cook the Omelette:

    Once the vegetables are cooked, spread them out evenly in the skillet.

Pour the beaten eggs over the vegetables, making sure they are evenly distributed.
Allow the eggs to cook undisturbed for a few minutes until the edges begin to set.

4. Add Cheese and Fold:

Sprinkle shredded cheese over one half of the omelette.
Using a spatula, carefully lift the other half of the omelette and fold it over the side with the cheese.
Press down gently with the spatula to seal the omelette.

5. Finish Cooking:

Continue cooking the omelette for another 1-2 minutes, or until the cheese is melted and the eggs are cooked through.
Slide the omelette onto a plate and garnish with fresh herbs, if desired.
Serve hot and enjoy your delicious vegetable omelette!

Vegetable omelettes are versatile and customizable, so feel free to experiment with different vegetables, cheeses, and seasonings to suit your taste preferences. They make a nutritious and satisfying breakfast, brunch, or even a quick and easy dinner option.

**Classic burger with lettuce, tomato, and onion**

Ingredients:

For the Burger Patties:

- 1 pound ground beef (80/20 blend for juicier burgers)
- Salt and pepper, to taste

For Assembling the Burger:

- 4 hamburger buns
- Lettuce leaves
- Tomato slices
- Onion slices
- Optional additional toppings: cheese slices, pickles, ketchup, mustard, mayonnaise

Instructions:

1. Prepare the Burger Patties:

    Divide the ground beef into 4 equal portions.
    Gently shape each portion into a patty, about 1/2 to 3/4 inch thick.
    Season both sides of the burger patties with salt and pepper to taste.

2. Cook the Burger Patties:

    Preheat a grill or a skillet over medium-high heat.
    If grilling, oil the grill grates. If using a skillet, add a little oil to the pan.
    Place the burger patties on the preheated grill or skillet.
    Cook the patties for about 3-4 minutes on each side for medium-rare, or longer to reach your desired level of doneness.
    If adding cheese, place a slice of cheese on each patty during the last minute of cooking and cover the grill or skillet to melt the cheese.

3. Toast the Burger Buns:

    While the burger patties are cooking, split the hamburger buns in half and place them cut-side down on the grill or skillet.

Toast the buns for 1-2 minutes, or until lightly golden and crisp.

4. Assemble the Burgers:

    Place a lettuce leaf on the bottom half of each toasted bun.
    Top the lettuce with a cooked burger patty.
    Add a slice of tomato and a few onion slices on top of each patty.
    Optionally, add any additional toppings of your choice, such as pickles, ketchup, mustard, or mayonnaise.
    Cover each burger with the top half of the toasted bun.

5. Serve:

    Serve the classic burgers immediately while hot, with your favorite side dishes like fries or potato salad.
    Enjoy your delicious homemade classic burgers with lettuce, tomato, and onion!

Feel free to customize your burgers with additional toppings and condiments according to your preferences. Serve them at cookouts, family gatherings, or any occasion for a crowd-pleasing meal.

**Shrimp Po' Boy sandwich**

Ingredients:

For the Shrimp:

- 1 pound large shrimp, peeled and deveined
- 1 cup buttermilk
- 1 cup all-purpose flour
- 1 teaspoon paprika
- 1/2 teaspoon garlic powder
- 1/2 teaspoon onion powder
- 1/2 teaspoon cayenne pepper (adjust to taste)
- Salt and pepper, to taste
- Vegetable oil, for frying

For the Remoulade Sauce:

- 1/2 cup mayonnaise
- 2 tablespoons Dijon mustard
- 2 tablespoons chopped pickles or relish
- 1 tablespoon chopped fresh parsley
- 1 tablespoon lemon juice
- 1 teaspoon hot sauce (adjust to taste)
- 1 clove garlic, minced
- Salt and pepper, to taste

For Assembling the Po' Boy:

- French bread rolls or baguette, cut into sandwich-sized portions
- Lettuce leaves
- Tomato slices
- Sliced pickles
- Lemon wedges, for serving

Instructions:

1. Prepare the Shrimp:

   In a bowl, combine the buttermilk with salt and pepper. Add the peeled and deveined shrimp and let them marinate for about 30 minutes in the refrigerator.
   In another bowl, mix together the flour, paprika, garlic powder, onion powder, cayenne pepper, salt, and pepper.
   Heat vegetable oil in a deep fryer or large skillet to 350°F (175°C).
   Remove the shrimp from the buttermilk, allowing any excess to drip off.
   Dredge the shrimp in the seasoned flour mixture, shaking off any excess.
   Fry the shrimp in batches for 2-3 minutes, or until golden brown and crispy.
   Remove the fried shrimp from the oil and drain them on a paper towel-lined plate.

2. Prepare the Remoulade Sauce:

   In a small bowl, whisk together the mayonnaise, Dijon mustard, chopped pickles, chopped parsley, lemon juice, hot sauce, minced garlic, salt, and pepper until well combined.
   Taste and adjust the seasoning according to your preference. Refrigerate until ready to use.

3. Assemble the Po' Boy:

   Slice the French bread rolls or baguette lengthwise, leaving one side attached.
   Spread a generous amount of remoulade sauce on both sides of the bread.
   Layer lettuce leaves, tomato slices, sliced pickles, and the fried shrimp on the bottom half of the bread.
   Squeeze lemon juice over the shrimp, if desired.
   Close the sandwich with the top half of the bread.
   Repeat the process for the remaining sandwiches.

4. Serve:

   Serve the Shrimp Po' Boy sandwiches immediately, with additional remoulade sauce on the side for dipping.
   Enjoy your homemade Shrimp Po' Boy sandwiches with a side of coleslaw, potato salad, or fries!

This flavorful and satisfying sandwich is perfect for lunch or dinner and is sure to be a hit with seafood lovers. Adjust the level of spice in the remoulade sauce and shrimp breading to suit your taste preferences.

**Spinach and feta omelette**

Ingredients:

- 3 large eggs
- Salt and pepper, to taste
- 1 tablespoon butter or olive oil
- 1 cup fresh spinach leaves, chopped
- 1/4 cup crumbled feta cheese
- Optional: chopped tomatoes, onions, mushrooms, or other vegetables of your choice

Instructions:

1. Prepare the Ingredients:

    Crack the eggs into a bowl and beat them until well combined. Season with salt and pepper to taste.
    Chop the fresh spinach leaves and any other vegetables you're using.

2. Cook the Spinach:

    Heat the butter or olive oil in a non-stick skillet over medium heat.
    Add the chopped spinach to the skillet and sauté for 1-2 minutes, or until wilted.

3. Add the Eggs:

    Pour the beaten eggs over the sautéed spinach in the skillet.
    Allow the eggs to cook undisturbed for a minute or two until the edges start to set.

4. Add the Feta Cheese:

    Sprinkle the crumbled feta cheese evenly over one half of the omelette.
    If using any additional vegetables, add them on top of the feta cheese.

5. Fold the Omelette:

Use a spatula to carefully lift one side of the omelette and fold it over the side with the filling.
Press down gently with the spatula to seal the omelette.

6. Finish Cooking:

Allow the omelette to cook for another minute or two until the cheese is melted and the eggs are cooked through.
Slide the omelette onto a plate and serve hot.

7. Serve:

Serve the spinach and feta omelette hot, garnished with additional freshly ground black pepper if desired.
Enjoy your delicious and nutritious breakfast!

This spinach and feta omelette is a great way to start your day with a healthy and satisfying meal. You can customize it by adding your favorite vegetables or herbs. Serve it with a side of toast or fresh fruit for a complete breakfast.

**Hot roast beef sandwich with gravy**

Ingredients:

For the Roast Beef:

- 1 pound beef roast (such as chuck or sirloin)
- Salt and pepper, to taste
- 2 tablespoons vegetable oil

For the Gravy:

- 2 tablespoons unsalted butter
- 2 tablespoons all-purpose flour
- 1 cup beef broth
- Salt and pepper, to taste

For Assembling the Sandwiches:

- Sliced bread or rolls (such as French bread or hoagie rolls)
- Prepared roast beef
- Prepared gravy

Instructions:

1. Prepare the Roast Beef:

>Preheat the oven to 325°F (160°C).
>Season the beef roast generously with salt and pepper.
>Heat vegetable oil in a large oven-safe skillet or Dutch oven over medium-high heat.
>Sear the seasoned beef roast on all sides until browned, about 4-5 minutes per side.
>Transfer the skillet or Dutch oven to the preheated oven and roast the beef for about 1-1.5 hours, or until it reaches your desired level of doneness (about 135°F or 57°C for medium-rare).

Remove the beef from the oven and let it rest for 10-15 minutes before slicing it thinly against the grain.

2. Prepare the Gravy:

   In a saucepan, melt the butter over medium heat.
   Stir in the flour to form a roux and cook for 1-2 minutes, stirring constantly.
   Gradually whisk in the beef broth until smooth.
   Bring the mixture to a simmer and cook for 3-4 minutes, or until the gravy thickens.
   Season with salt and pepper to taste.

3. Assemble the Sandwiches:

   Slice the bread or rolls in half and toast them if desired.
   Place slices of the prepared roast beef on one half of each sandwich.
   Pour warm gravy over the roast beef.
   Top with the other half of the bread or roll.

4. Serve:

   Serve the hot roast beef sandwiches with gravy immediately.
   Optionally, serve with mashed potatoes, coleslaw, or a side salad.
   Enjoy your comforting and delicious hot roast beef sandwiches!

These hot roast beef sandwiches with gravy are perfect for a cozy dinner or lunch.

They're sure to be a hit with family and friends, especially on chilly days when you're craving something hearty and comforting.

**Cobb salad**

Ingredients:

For the Salad:

- 6 cups mixed salad greens (such as romaine, iceberg, and arugula)
- 2 cooked chicken breasts, diced or sliced
- 8 slices bacon, cooked until crispy and chopped
- 2 hard-boiled eggs, chopped
- 1 large ripe avocado, diced
- 1 cup cherry tomatoes, halved
- 1/2 cup crumbled blue cheese or feta cheese
- 1/4 cup sliced green onions (optional)
- Salt and pepper, to taste

For the Dressing:

- 1/2 cup mayonnaise
- 2 tablespoons red wine vinegar
- 1 teaspoon Dijon mustard
- 1 clove garlic, minced
- Salt and pepper, to taste

Instructions:

1. Prepare the Salad:

    Arrange the mixed salad greens in a large salad bowl or on a serving platter. Arrange the diced or sliced cooked chicken breast, chopped bacon, chopped hard-boiled eggs, diced avocado, halved cherry tomatoes, crumbled blue cheese (or feta cheese), and sliced green onions (if using) in rows or sections over the salad greens.
    Season the salad with salt and pepper, to taste.

2. Prepare the Dressing:

In a small bowl, whisk together the mayonnaise, red wine vinegar, Dijon mustard, minced garlic, salt, and pepper until smooth and well combined.
Taste and adjust the seasoning, adding more salt and pepper if needed.

3. Serve:

Drizzle the prepared dressing over the Cobb salad just before serving, or serve the dressing on the side.
Toss the salad gently to coat the ingredients with the dressing.
Serve immediately and enjoy your delicious Cobb salad!

Cobb salad is a versatile dish, so feel free to customize it with your favorite ingredients or substitutions. You can add grilled shrimp, turkey, or even salmon instead of chicken.

It's perfect for a light lunch or dinner and is sure to be a hit with family and friends.

**Turkey burger with sweet potato fries**

Turkey Burger Ingredients:

- 1 lb ground turkey
- 1/4 cup breadcrumbs
- 1/4 cup grated Parmesan cheese
- 1/4 cup finely chopped onion
- 1 clove garlic, minced
- 1 tablespoon Worcestershire sauce
- 1 teaspoon dried parsley
- 1/2 teaspoon dried basil
- Salt and pepper to taste
- Burger buns
- Lettuce leaves, tomato slices, sliced onions, pickles (for garnish)

Sweet Potato Fries Ingredients:

- 2 large sweet potatoes
- 2 tablespoons olive oil
- 1 teaspoon paprika
- 1/2 teaspoon garlic powder
- Salt and pepper to taste

Instructions:

1. Prepare the Turkey Burgers:

> In a large bowl, combine the ground turkey, breadcrumbs, grated Parmesan cheese, chopped onion, minced garlic, Worcestershire sauce, dried parsley, dried basil, salt, and pepper.
> Mix all ingredients until well combined. Be careful not to overwork the mixture.
> Divide the mixture into equal portions and shape them into patties.
> Preheat a grill or skillet over medium heat. If using a skillet, add a little oil to prevent sticking.
> Cook the turkey patties for about 5-6 minutes on each side, or until they are cooked through and reach an internal temperature of 165°F (74°C).

Remove the patties from the grill or skillet and let them rest for a few minutes.

2. Prepare the Sweet Potato Fries:

Preheat your oven to 425°F (220°C) and line a baking sheet with parchment paper.
Peel the sweet potatoes and cut them into thin strips, resembling fries.
In a large bowl, toss the sweet potato fries with olive oil, paprika, garlic powder, salt, and pepper until evenly coated.
Spread the fries in a single layer on the prepared baking sheet.
Bake in the preheated oven for 20-25 minutes, flipping halfway through, until the fries are golden brown and crispy.

3. Assemble the Burgers:

Toast the burger buns lightly, if desired.
Place a turkey burger patty on the bottom half of each bun.
Top with lettuce leaves, tomato slices, sliced onions, and pickles, as desired.
Place the top half of the bun over the toppings to complete the burger.
Serve the turkey burgers with sweet potato fries on the side.
Enjoy your delicious and healthier turkey burger with sweet potato fries!

Feel free to customize your turkey burgers with your favorite toppings and condiments.

You can also serve them with a side of salad or coleslaw for a complete meal.

**Greek salad**

Ingredients:

For the Salad:

- 4 cups chopped romaine lettuce or mixed salad greens
- 1 large cucumber, diced
- 1 cup cherry tomatoes, halved
- 1/2 red onion, thinly sliced
- 1/2 cup pitted Kalamata olives
- 1/2 cup crumbled feta cheese
- Optional: chopped red bell pepper, chopped green bell pepper, sliced pepperoncini peppers, sliced radishes

For the Dressing:

- 1/4 cup extra virgin olive oil
- 2 tablespoons red wine vinegar
- 1 clove garlic, minced
- 1 teaspoon dried oregano
- Salt and pepper, to taste

Instructions:

1. Prepare the Salad:

    In a large salad bowl, combine the chopped romaine lettuce or mixed salad greens, diced cucumber, halved cherry tomatoes, thinly sliced red onion, Kalamata olives, and crumbled feta cheese.
    Add any optional ingredients, such as chopped bell peppers, pepperoncini peppers, or radishes, if desired.
    Toss the salad gently to combine all the ingredients.

2. Prepare the Dressing:

    In a small bowl, whisk together the extra virgin olive oil, red wine vinegar, minced garlic, dried oregano, salt, and pepper until well combined.
    Taste and adjust the seasoning, adding more salt and pepper if needed.

3. Serve:

> Drizzle the prepared dressing over the Greek salad just before serving.
> Toss the salad gently to coat the vegetables and cheese with the dressing.
> Serve the Greek salad immediately as a side dish or as a light and refreshing main course.
> Enjoy your delicious homemade Greek salad!

Greek salad is perfect for a summer barbecue, potluck, or as a side dish with grilled meats or seafood. It's also a great option for a light and healthy lunch. Feel free to customize your Greek salad by adding your favorite ingredients or adjusting the dressing to suit your taste preferences.

**Classic meatloaf sandwich**

Ingredients:

For the Meatloaf:

- 1 pound ground beef
- 1/2 cup breadcrumbs
- 1/4 cup milk
- 1 egg
- 1/4 cup finely chopped onion
- 1/4 cup finely chopped green bell pepper
- 2 cloves garlic, minced
- 2 tablespoons ketchup
- 1 tablespoon Worcestershire sauce
- 1 teaspoon dried parsley
- 1/2 teaspoon salt
- 1/4 teaspoon black pepper

For the Sandwich:

- Sliced sandwich bread or hamburger buns
- Lettuce leaves
- Sliced tomato
- Sliced onion
- Pickles
- Ketchup, mustard, mayonnaise (optional)

Instructions:

1. Prepare the Meatloaf:

> Preheat your oven to 350°F (175°C).
> In a large mixing bowl, combine the ground beef, breadcrumbs, milk, egg, chopped onion, chopped bell pepper, minced garlic, ketchup, Worcestershire sauce, dried parsley, salt, and black pepper.
> Mix all the ingredients together until well combined.

Transfer the mixture to a loaf pan and press it down evenly.
Bake in the preheated oven for about 45-55 minutes, or until the meatloaf is cooked through and reaches an internal temperature of 160°F (71°C).
Remove the meatloaf from the oven and let it rest for a few minutes before slicing.

2. Assemble the Sandwich:

Slice the meatloaf into thick slices.
Toast the sandwich bread or hamburger buns, if desired.
Place a slice of meatloaf on one slice of bread or the bottom half of a hamburger bun.
Top the meatloaf with lettuce leaves, sliced tomato, sliced onion, and pickles.
Add ketchup, mustard, or mayonnaise, if desired.
Place the other slice of bread or the top half of the hamburger bun over the toppings to complete the sandwich.

3. Serve:

Serve the classic meatloaf sandwich immediately, with your favorite side dishes like potato chips, coleslaw, or a salad.
Enjoy your delicious and comforting meatloaf sandwich!

Feel free to customize your meatloaf sandwich with additional toppings or condiments according to your preferences. You can also add cheese slices or bacon for extra flavor. It's a versatile and satisfying meal that's sure to be a hit with family and friends.

**Chicken Caesar wrap**

Ingredients:

For the Chicken:

- 2 boneless, skinless chicken breasts
- Salt and pepper, to taste
- 1 tablespoon olive oil

For the Caesar Dressing:

- 1/2 cup mayonnaise
- 2 tablespoons grated Parmesan cheese
- 1 tablespoon lemon juice
- 1 teaspoon Dijon mustard
- 1 clove garlic, minced
- 1/2 teaspoon Worcestershire sauce
- Salt and pepper, to taste

For the Wrap:

- 4 large flour tortillas
- Romaine lettuce leaves
- Shredded Parmesan cheese
- Croutons (store-bought or homemade)
- Optional: sliced cherry tomatoes, cooked bacon, avocado slices

Instructions:

1. Prepare the Chicken:

> Season the chicken breasts with salt and pepper on both sides.
> Heat olive oil in a skillet over medium-high heat.
> Add the seasoned chicken breasts to the skillet and cook for 6-8 minutes per side, or until they are cooked through and no longer pink in the center.

Remove the chicken from the skillet and let it rest for a few minutes before slicing it into strips or cubes.

2. Make the Caesar Dressing:

In a small bowl, whisk together the mayonnaise, grated Parmesan cheese, lemon juice, Dijon mustard, minced garlic, Worcestershire sauce, salt, and pepper until smooth and well combined.
Taste and adjust the seasoning, adding more salt and pepper if needed.

3. Assemble the Wraps:

Lay out the flour tortillas on a clean surface.
Spread a generous amount of Caesar dressing over each tortilla, leaving a border around the edges.
Place a layer of romaine lettuce leaves over the dressing on each tortilla.
Arrange the sliced chicken evenly over the lettuce.
Sprinkle shredded Parmesan cheese over the chicken.
Add croutons on top for crunch.
Optionally, add sliced cherry tomatoes, cooked bacon, or avocado slices.

4. Wrap the Wraps:

Fold the sides of each tortilla inward, then roll it up tightly from the bottom to form a wrap.
Cut each wrap in half diagonally, if desired, for easier handling.

5. Serve:

Serve the Chicken Caesar wraps immediately, or wrap them tightly in foil or parchment paper for later.
Enjoy your delicious and portable Chicken Caesar wraps as a quick and easy meal on the go or for a light lunch or dinner!

Feel free to customize your Chicken Caesar wraps by adding your favorite ingredients or adjusting the amount of dressing according to your taste preferences. They're versatile, satisfying, and perfect for any occasion.

**Grilled salmon with steamed vegetables**

Ingredients:

For the Grilled Salmon:

- 4 salmon fillets (about 6 ounces each), skin-on or skinless
- 2 tablespoons olive oil
- Salt and pepper, to taste
- Lemon wedges, for serving

For the Steamed Vegetables:

- Assorted vegetables of your choice, such as broccoli, carrots, zucchini, bell peppers, and snap peas
- Salt and pepper, to taste
- Butter or olive oil, for drizzling (optional)
- Fresh herbs, such as parsley or dill, for garnish (optional)

Instructions:

1. Prepare the Salmon:

    Preheat your grill to medium-high heat.
    Pat the salmon fillets dry with paper towels and brush them with olive oil on both sides.
    Season the salmon fillets generously with salt and pepper.
    Place the salmon fillets on the preheated grill, skin-side down if they have skin.
    Grill the salmon for about 4-5 minutes per side, depending on the thickness of the fillets, or until they are cooked through and easily flake with a fork.
    Remove the grilled salmon from the grill and transfer them to a serving platter.
    Squeeze fresh lemon juice over the grilled salmon fillets just before serving.

2. Steam the Vegetables:

    While the salmon is grilling, prepare the vegetables.
    Wash and chop the assorted vegetables into bite-sized pieces.

Fill a large pot with about an inch of water and place a steamer basket inside.
Bring the water to a boil over medium-high heat.
Add the chopped vegetables to the steamer basket, season with salt and pepper to taste, and cover the pot with a lid.
Steam the vegetables for about 5-7 minutes, or until they are tender but still crisp.
Remove the steamed vegetables from the pot and transfer them to a serving dish.
Drizzle with a little butter or olive oil, if desired, and garnish with fresh herbs.

3. Serve:

Serve the grilled salmon fillets alongside the steamed vegetables.
Optionally, garnish the salmon with additional lemon wedges and fresh herbs.
Enjoy your delicious and healthy grilled salmon with steamed vegetables!

This dish is not only nutritious and flavorful but also versatile. Feel free to customize it by using your favorite vegetables or adding your preferred seasonings and sauces. It's a perfect meal for a quick weeknight dinner or a special occasion.

**Meatball sub**

Ingredients:

For the Meatballs:

- 1 pound ground beef
- 1/2 cup breadcrumbs
- 1/4 cup grated Parmesan cheese
- 1 egg
- 2 cloves garlic, minced
- 1 teaspoon dried oregano
- 1 teaspoon dried basil
- Salt and pepper, to taste
- Olive oil, for cooking

For the Marinara Sauce:

- 1 (14 oz) can crushed tomatoes
- 2 cloves garlic, minced
- 1 teaspoon dried oregano
- 1 teaspoon dried basil
- Salt and pepper, to taste

For the Sub:

- 4 sub rolls or hoagie rolls
- Mozzarella cheese, shredded or sliced
- Fresh parsley, chopped (for garnish, optional)

Instructions:

1. Make the Meatballs:

    Preheat your oven to 375°F (190°C).

In a large mixing bowl, combine the ground beef, breadcrumbs, grated Parmesan cheese, egg, minced garlic, dried oregano, dried basil, salt, and pepper. Mix until well combined.

Roll the mixture into meatballs, about 1 to 1.5 inches in diameter.

Heat olive oil in a skillet over medium heat. Once hot, add the meatballs and cook until browned on all sides, about 5-7 minutes.

Transfer the browned meatballs to a baking sheet lined with parchment paper.

Bake in the preheated oven for 10-12 minutes, or until cooked through.

2. Prepare the Marinara Sauce:

In the same skillet used for cooking the meatballs, add a little more olive oil if needed.

Add the minced garlic and sauté until fragrant, about 1 minute.

Stir in the crushed tomatoes, dried oregano, dried basil, salt, and pepper. Bring to a simmer and cook for 5-10 minutes, until slightly thickened.

3. Assemble the Subs:

Slice the sub rolls in half lengthwise, leaving one side attached.

Place a layer of shredded or sliced mozzarella cheese on the bottom half of each roll.

Spoon some marinara sauce over the cheese.

Add a few meatballs on top of the sauce.

Spoon a little more marinara sauce over the meatballs.

If desired, sprinkle with additional shredded mozzarella cheese.

Place the top half of each sub roll over the filling.

4. Serve:

Place the assembled meatball subs on a baking sheet and return them to the oven for a few minutes to melt the cheese.

Garnish with chopped fresh parsley, if desired.

Serve hot and enjoy your delicious meatball subs!

These meatball subs are perfect for a quick and easy dinner or lunch. They're sure to be a hit with the whole family!

**Greek omelette**

Ingredients:

- 3 large eggs
- 1/4 cup crumbled feta cheese
- 1/4 cup chopped tomatoes
- 1/4 cup chopped spinach
- 1/4 cup chopped red onion
- 2 tablespoons chopped black olives
- 1 tablespoon chopped fresh parsley
- Salt and pepper, to taste
- Olive oil or butter, for cooking

Instructions:

1. Prepare the Ingredients:

    Crack the eggs into a mixing bowl and beat them until well combined.
    Chop the tomatoes, spinach, red onion, black olives, and fresh parsley.

2. Cook the Omelette:

    Heat a little olive oil or butter in a non-stick skillet over medium heat.
    Pour the beaten eggs into the skillet, swirling to spread them evenly.
    Let the eggs cook for a minute or two until the edges start to set.
    Sprinkle the crumbled feta cheese evenly over one half of the omelette.
    Add the chopped tomatoes, spinach, red onion, black olives, and fresh parsley on top of the feta cheese.
    Season with salt and pepper, to taste.

3. Fold the Omelette:

    Use a spatula to carefully lift one side of the omelette and fold it over the side with the filling.
    Press down gently with the spatula to seal the omelette.

Let the omelette cook for another minute or two until the cheese is melted and the eggs are cooked through.

4. Serve:

Slide the Greek omelette onto a plate and serve hot.
Optionally, garnish with additional chopped parsley or a sprinkle of crumbled feta cheese.
Enjoy your delicious and nutritious Greek omelette!

This Greek omelette is packed with flavor from the feta cheese, tomatoes, spinach, olives, and fresh herbs. It's a satisfying breakfast option that's easy to customize with your favorite ingredients. Serve it with a side of toast or a Greek salad for a complete meal.

**Classic tuna salad sandwich**

Ingredients:

For the Tuna Salad:

- 2 cans (5 ounces each) of tuna in water, drained
- 1/4 cup mayonnaise
- 1 tablespoon Dijon mustard
- 1 celery stalk, finely chopped
- 2 tablespoons finely chopped red onion
- 2 tablespoons chopped fresh parsley (optional)
- Salt and pepper, to taste
- Lemon juice (optional, for added freshness)

For the Sandwich:

- Sliced bread of your choice (white, whole wheat, or multi-grain)
- Lettuce leaves
- Sliced tomato
- Sliced cucumber (optional)
- Sliced avocado (optional)

Instructions:

1. Prepare the Tuna Salad:

    In a mixing bowl, combine the drained tuna, mayonnaise, Dijon mustard, chopped celery, chopped red onion, and chopped parsley (if using).
    Mix all the ingredients together until well combined.
    Season the tuna salad with salt and pepper to taste.
    Optionally, add a squeeze of lemon juice for added freshness.

2. Assemble the Sandwich:

    Lay out the slices of bread on a clean surface.
    Place a lettuce leaf on one slice of bread.
    Spoon the tuna salad mixture evenly onto the lettuce.
    Top the tuna salad with slices of tomato, cucumber (if using), and avocado (if using).

Place another slice of bread on top to complete the sandwich.

3. Serve:

   Cut the sandwich in half diagonally, if desired.
   Serve the classic tuna salad sandwich immediately, or wrap it tightly in foil or plastic wrap for later.
   Enjoy your delicious and satisfying classic tuna salad sandwich!

Feel free to customize your tuna salad sandwich with your favorite ingredients or condiments. You can add chopped pickles, olives, or capers for extra flavor, or use different types of bread for variety. It's a versatile and convenient meal that's perfect for lunch or a quick dinner.

**BBQ pulled pork sandwich**

Ingredients:

For the Pulled Pork:

- 3-4 pounds pork shoulder or pork butt
- Salt and pepper, to taste
- 1 tablespoon olive oil
- 1 onion, sliced
- 3 cloves garlic, minced
- 1 cup chicken or vegetable broth
- 1 cup barbecue sauce (store-bought or homemade)

For the Sandwiches:

- Hamburger buns or sandwich rolls
- Coleslaw (optional, for topping)
- Pickles (optional, for topping)
- Sliced onions (optional, for topping)

Instructions:

1. Prepare the Pulled Pork:

Season the pork shoulder or pork butt generously with salt and pepper.
Heat olive oil in a large skillet or Dutch oven over medium-high heat.
Sear the seasoned pork on all sides until browned, about 3-4 minutes per side.
Transfer the seared pork to a slow cooker or Instant Pot.
Add sliced onion and minced garlic to the skillet and sauté until softened, about 2-3 minutes.
Pour chicken or vegetable broth into the skillet and deglaze the bottom, scraping up any browned bits.
Pour the onion and garlic mixture over the pork in the slow cooker or Instant Pot.
Cover and cook on low heat for 8 hours in the slow cooker or high pressure for 90 minutes in the Instant Pot, until the pork is tender and easily shreds with a fork.

Once cooked, remove the pork from the slow cooker or Instant Pot and shred it using two forks.

Mix the shredded pork with barbecue sauce until well coated.

2. Assemble the Sandwiches:

Toast the hamburger buns or sandwich rolls, if desired.

Place a generous amount of pulled pork on the bottom half of each bun.

Top the pulled pork with coleslaw, pickles, sliced onions, or any other desired toppings.

Place the top half of the bun over the filling to complete the sandwich.

3. Serve:

Serve the BBQ pulled pork sandwiches immediately, accompanied by additional barbecue sauce on the side if desired.

Enjoy your delicious and hearty BBQ pulled pork sandwiches!

These BBQ pulled pork sandwiches are perfect for a casual dinner, barbecue, or potluck gathering. They're flavorful, tender, and sure to be a hit with family and friends.

**Cobb salad wrap**

Ingredients:

For the Salad:

- 2 cups chopped romaine lettuce
- 1/2 cup cooked chicken breast, diced
- 2 slices cooked bacon, crumbled
- 1 hard-boiled egg, chopped
- 1/2 avocado, diced
- 1/4 cup cherry tomatoes, halved
- 1/4 cup crumbled blue cheese
- 2 tablespoons chopped green onions
- Salt and pepper, to taste

For the Dressing:

- 2 tablespoons mayonnaise
- 1 tablespoon Greek yogurt (or sour cream)
- 1 tablespoon lemon juice
- 1 teaspoon Dijon mustard
- Salt and pepper, to taste

For the Wrap:

- 4 large flour tortillas or wraps

Instructions:

1. Prepare the Salad:

   In a large mixing bowl, combine the chopped romaine lettuce, diced chicken breast, crumbled bacon, chopped hard-boiled egg, diced avocado, cherry tomatoes, crumbled blue cheese, and chopped green onions.
   Season with salt and pepper, to taste. Toss until well combined.

2. Make the Dressing:

   In a small bowl, whisk together the mayonnaise, Greek yogurt (or sour cream), lemon juice, Dijon mustard, salt, and pepper until smooth and well combined.

3. Assemble the Wraps:

   Lay out the flour tortillas or wraps on a clean surface.
   Spread a generous amount of the prepared dressing over each tortilla, leaving a border around the edges.
   Spoon the prepared Cobb salad mixture evenly onto each tortilla.
   Roll up the tortillas tightly to form wraps, tucking in the sides as you go.

4. Serve:

   Slice each wrap in half diagonally, if desired.
   Serve the Cobb salad wraps immediately, or wrap them tightly in foil or plastic wrap for later.
   Enjoy your delicious and portable Cobb salad wraps!

These Cobb salad wraps are perfect for a quick and easy lunch or dinner. They're packed with flavor and nutrients, making them a satisfying and healthy meal option. Feel free to customize the wraps with your favorite salad ingredients or add additional toppings to suit your taste preferences.

**Spinach and mushroom omelette**

Ingredients:

- 2 large eggs
- 1/4 cup chopped mushrooms
- 1/4 cup fresh spinach leaves, chopped
- 1/4 cup shredded cheese (such as cheddar, mozzarella, or feta)
- 1 tablespoon butter or olive oil
- Salt and pepper, to taste
- Optional: chopped onion, bell pepper, tomato, or any other vegetables of your choice

Instructions:

1. Prepare the Ingredients:

    Crack the eggs into a mixing bowl and beat them until well combined. Season with salt and pepper, to taste.
    Chop the mushrooms and spinach leaves. If using any other vegetables, chop them as well.

2. Cook the Vegetables:

    Heat butter or olive oil in a non-stick skillet over medium heat.
    Add the chopped mushrooms to the skillet and cook for 2-3 minutes, until they start to soften.
    Add the chopped spinach to the skillet and cook for another 1-2 minutes, until wilted.
    If using any other vegetables, add them to the skillet and cook until softened.

3. Make the Omelette:

    Pour the beaten eggs into the skillet over the cooked vegetables.
    Use a spatula to gently lift the edges of the omelette as it cooks, allowing the uncooked eggs to flow underneath.

When the eggs are mostly set but still slightly runny on top, sprinkle the shredded cheese evenly over one half of the omelette.
Cook for another minute or until the cheese starts to melt.
Use the spatula to fold the other half of the omelette over the cheese-covered half, forming a half-moon shape.
Press down gently with the spatula to seal the omelette.

4. Serve:

Slide the spinach and mushroom omelette onto a plate.
Garnish with additional shredded cheese or chopped herbs, if desired.
Serve hot and enjoy your delicious and nutritious omelette!

This spinach and mushroom omelette is versatile, so feel free to customize it with your favorite ingredients or seasonings. You can serve it with toast, a side salad, or fresh fruit for a complete meal. It's a satisfying breakfast option that's packed with protein and nutrients.

**Veggie burger with coleslaw**

Ingredients:

For the Veggie Burger Patties:

- 1 can (15 ounces) black beans, drained and rinsed
- 1/2 cup cooked quinoa or breadcrumbs
- 1/4 cup finely chopped onion
- 1/4 cup finely chopped bell pepper (any color)
- 2 cloves garlic, minced
- 1 teaspoon ground cumin
- 1 teaspoon smoked paprika
- Salt and pepper, to taste
- Olive oil, for cooking

For the Coleslaw:

- 2 cups shredded cabbage (green or purple)
- 1 carrot, grated
- 1/4 cup mayonnaise
- 1 tablespoon apple cider vinegar
- 1 teaspoon honey or sugar
- Salt and pepper, to taste

For Serving:

- Burger buns
- Lettuce leaves
- Sliced tomato
- Sliced avocado (optional)

Instructions:

1. Make the Veggie Burger Patties:

In a large mixing bowl, mash the black beans using a fork or potato masher until mostly smooth.

Add the cooked quinoa or breadcrumbs, chopped onion, chopped bell pepper, minced garlic, ground cumin, smoked paprika, salt, and pepper to the mashed black beans. Mix until well combined.

Divide the mixture into 4 equal portions and shape them into burger patties.

Heat a little olive oil in a skillet over medium heat. Once hot, add the burger patties to the skillet.

Cook the patties for about 4-5 minutes on each side, or until they are golden brown and heated through.

2. Make the Coleslaw:

In a large mixing bowl, combine the shredded cabbage and grated carrot.

In a small bowl, whisk together the mayonnaise, apple cider vinegar, honey or sugar, salt, and pepper until smooth and well combined.

Pour the dressing over the cabbage and carrot mixture. Toss until the vegetables are evenly coated with the dressing.

3. Assemble the Veggie Burgers:

Toast the burger buns, if desired.

Place a lettuce leaf on the bottom half of each bun.

Place a veggie burger patty on top of the lettuce.

Top the burger patty with a spoonful of coleslaw.

Add sliced tomato and sliced avocado, if desired.

Place the top half of each bun over the filling to complete the burgers.

4. Serve:

Serve the veggie burgers with coleslaw immediately.

Enjoy your delicious and hearty veggie burger with coleslaw!

These veggie burgers with coleslaw are packed with flavor and nutrients, making them a perfect vegetarian meal option. They're great for lunch or dinner and can be customized with your favorite toppings and condiments.

**Steak and eggs**

Ingredients:

For the Steak:

- 2 boneless ribeye steaks (about 8 ounces each)
- Salt and pepper, to taste
- 1 tablespoon olive oil or butter

For the Eggs:

- 4 large eggs
- Salt and pepper, to taste
- Butter, for cooking

Optional Garnishes:

- Chopped fresh parsley or chives
- Sliced avocado
- Sliced tomatoes
- Hot sauce or steak sauce

Instructions:

1. Prepare the Steak:

    Season the ribeye steaks generously with salt and pepper on both sides. Heat olive oil or butter in a skillet over medium-high heat until hot. Add the seasoned steaks to the skillet and cook to your desired doneness, flipping once halfway through cooking. For medium-rare, cook for about 3-4 minutes per side, or adjust the cooking time according to your preference. Once cooked to your liking, remove the steaks from the skillet and let them rest for a few minutes before serving.

2. Cook the Eggs:

In the same skillet used to cook the steaks, lower the heat to medium.
Add a little more butter to the skillet if needed.
Crack the eggs into the skillet and season with salt and pepper to taste.
Cook the eggs to your preference – sunny-side up, over-easy, or scrambled.

3. Serve:

Transfer the cooked steaks to plates.
Place the cooked eggs on top of the steaks.
Garnish with chopped fresh parsley or chives, if desired.
Serve immediately with optional garnishes like sliced avocado, sliced tomatoes, and hot sauce or steak sauce on the side.
Enjoy your delicious and hearty steak and eggs breakfast or brunch!

Feel free to customize your steak and eggs by adding your favorite sides such as toast, hash browns, or sautéed vegetables. It's a satisfying and protein-packed dish that's perfect for any time of day.

**Classic chocolate milkshake**

Ingredients:

- 2 cups vanilla ice cream
- 1/2 cup milk (adjust according to desired thickness)
- 2 tablespoons chocolate syrup
- Whipped cream (optional, for topping)
- Maraschino cherry (optional, for garnish)

Instructions:

Add the vanilla ice cream, milk, and chocolate syrup to a blender.
Blend until smooth and creamy. If the milkshake is too thick, add more milk, a little at a time, until you reach your desired consistency.
Pour the chocolate milkshake into glasses.
Optionally, top with whipped cream and garnish with a maraschino cherry.
Serve immediately with a straw and enjoy your classic chocolate milkshake!

Feel free to customize your chocolate milkshake by adding toppings like chocolate shavings, crushed cookies, or sprinkles. You can also experiment with different flavors of ice cream or add-ins like peanut butter or mint extract for a twist on the classic recipe.

www.ingramcontent.com/pod-product-compliance
Lightning Source LLC
LaVergne TN
LVHW081559060526
838201LV00054B/1977